Alfred's Premier Piano Course

Dennis Alexander • Gayle Kowalchyk • E. L. Lancaster • Victoria McArthur • Martha Mier

Edited by Morton Manus

Cover Design by Ted Engelbart
Interior Design by Tom Gerou
Illustrations by Jimmy Holder
Music Engraving by Linda Lusk

ISBN-10: 0-7390-4543-1
ISBN-13: 978-0-7390-4543-5

Contents

A Note to Teachers. 2

A Note to Students (and Parents) 3

Technique Tool 1 *(Relaxed Shoulders)*. 3

Technique Tool 2 *(Arm Weight)*. 4

Technique Tool 3 *(Moving Freely)* 5

Technique Tool 4 *(Strong Fingertips)* 6

Technique Tool 5 *(Finger Weights)* 8

Artistic Etude 1 *(Playing with a Steady Pulse)* 9

Technique Tool 6 *(Repeated Notes)* 10

Technique Tool 7 *(Thumb Position)* 11

Technique Tool 8 *(Finger Independence)* 13

Artistic Etude 2 *(Playing Across the Bar Line)* 14

Patterns in Music 16

Artistic Etude 3 *(Playing Evenly from Hand to Hand)* 20

Artistic Etude 4 *(Playing with Dynamics)* 26

Technique Tool 9 *(Gentle Hand Rock)* 29

Artistic Etude 5 *(Moods in Music)* 30

Technique Tool Review. 32

A Note to Teachers

The art of playing the piano requires three things: knowledge, musical feeling, and the physical skills to perform what is artistically intended, also known as technique. The development of technique is essential to future success at the piano. Developing technique is a result of first understanding, then practicing the correct physical movements many times.

The Technique Books of *Alfred's Premier Piano Course* give students the technical tools needed to achieve artistic performances. Each page in the Technique Book correlates with a specific page in the Lesson Book. When the Lesson, Theory, Performance and Technique books are used together, they offer a fully-integrated and unparalleled comprehensive approach to piano instruction.

In Technique Book 1A, students encounter technical skills in four areas:

Playing Naturally

Students will always remain aware of basic relaxed body posture and hand position. In addition, students will work on:

1. arm weight for a more beautiful sound while playing effortlessly.
2. strong fingertips for control of sound.
3. thumb position and finger independence to use all fingers equally well.
4. gentle hand rock to promote relaxed physical motion.

Moving Freely

Students will learn to move around the keyboard with freedom and ease.

Playing Beautifully

Students will learn to produce changes in dynamics and tone by:

1. controlling and varying the weight into the keys.
2. staying close to the key surface. while playing repeated notes.

Playing Artistically

Students will learn to play artistically by:

1. playing steadily across the bar line.
2. using dynamics to create varied colors in music.
3. moving smoothly from hand to hand while playing evenly.
4. creating moods with music.

To achieve these skills, technical principles are clearly identified and named on each page.

The technical goals are accomplished through three types of activities in *Technique Book 1A*:

Technique Tools clearly present the following technical goals through appealing and descriptive exercises:

1. *Relaxed Shoulders* (p. 3)
2. *Arm Weight* (p. 4)
3. *Moving Freely* (p. 5)
4. *Strong Fingertips* (p. 6)
5. *Finger Weights* (p. 8)
6. *Repeated Notes* (p. 10)
7. *Thumb Position* (p. 11)
8. *Finger Independence* (p. 13)
9. *Gentle Hand Rock* (p. 29)

These Technique Tools should always be introduced to the student during the lesson. Visit PremierPianoCourse.com to see a video demonstration of each Technique Tool.

Patterned Exercises provide students with the necessary repetitions to make the technique feel natural. Memorization, although optional, is suggested.

Artistic Etudes showcase a student's technique in an artistic musical setting, with a duet.

The overall goal of the Technique Books in *Alfred's Premier Piano Course* is to develop the physical skills needed to play artistically, expressively and effortlessly.

Use with *Alfred's Premier Lesson Book Level 1A*, pages 4–5

A Note to Students (and Parents)

Piano technique is about:

- The way you use your body, arms, wrists, hands and fingers at the keyboard.
- How you move freely around the keyboard.
- The sounds (also called tones) you create at the keyboard.

Outstanding artists, athletes and dancers all practice their technique so they can be successful and improve their skills. You'll find that practicing piano technique regularly will improve your skills, as well.

Just like star athletes and professional dancers, it is important to warm up each day by working on technique first.

Show your teacher your best piano technique as you:

- Check the height of the piano bench.
- Check your distance from the keyboard.
- Check your posture.
- Find a good hand position.

If you need to review, see Lesson Book 1A, pages 4–5.

Technique Tool 1*

Relaxed Shoulders

- Sit up straight yet relaxed on the piano bench. Let your relaxed and heavy arms hang straight down.
- Raise your shoulders up toward your ears as you take a deep breath.
- Relax, breathe out, and let your shoulders fall back down into a natural position before playing.

Repeat 3 times each day.

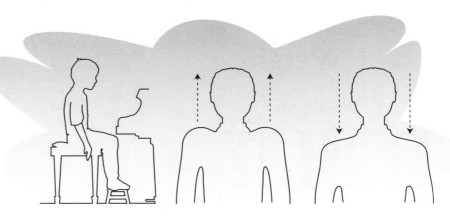

* **Note to Teacher:** The first 13 pages of the book introduce Technique Tools 1–8. Technique Tool 9 is found on page 29.

4

Technique Tool 2

Arm Weight

- On the closed keyboard cover, place both hands in a playing position.
- Slowly raise your hands and arms up to chin level.
- Imagine that your arms are heavy as you suddenly *let go*, dropping your hands onto your lap.
- Repeat, but this time drop your relaxed hands, landing on the closed keyboard cover.
- Your hands should feel relaxed and heavy as they drop.

Repeat 3 times each day.

✔ **Technique Tip:** In "Great Weight," use *arm weight* to play with a full sound.

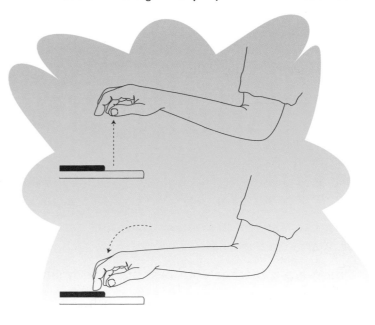

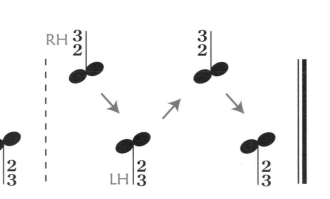

Great Weight*

Hand Position

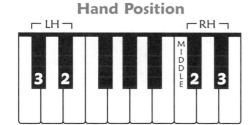

Play loud.

* Titles of exercises throughout the book suggest imagery that will help the student understand the technical concepts.

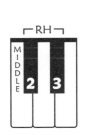

Technique Tool 3

Moving Freely

- LH: With your left hand and arm, gently trace a *curved arch* like a rainbow moving *down* the keyboard.

- Play "Beautiful Arches (LH)" on the closed keyboard cover as your left hand gently drops onto the wood.

- RH: With your right hand and arm, gently trace a *curved arch* like a rainbow moving *up* the keyboard.

- Play "Beautiful Arches (RH)" on the closed keyboard cover as your right hand gently drops onto the wood.

Repeat 3 times each day with LH, then RH.

Technique Tip: In "Beautiful Arches," *move freely* up and down the keyboard, using gentle, curved arches.

Beautiful Arches (LH)

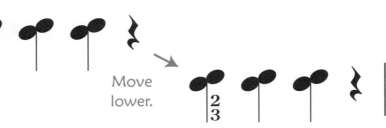

Play moderately (medium) loud.

LH | 2 3

Move lower to next 2-black-key group.

Move lower.

Beautiful Arches (RH)

Play moderately (medium) loud.

RH 3 2

Move higher to next 2-black-key group.

Move higher.

6

Technique Tool 4

Strong Fingertips (LH)

- Place the LH in a rounded hand position on the closed keyboard cover.
- Keeping each joint firm, imagine that your fingertips are very strong as you tap LH fingers 2, 3 and 4 on each fingertip pad.
- Start with LH finger 2 and tap each finger 4 times.*

Repeat 3 times each day.

Technique Tip: In "Pumping Iron (LH)," use *strong* LH *fingertips*. Use *arm weight* and *move freely* on the second line.

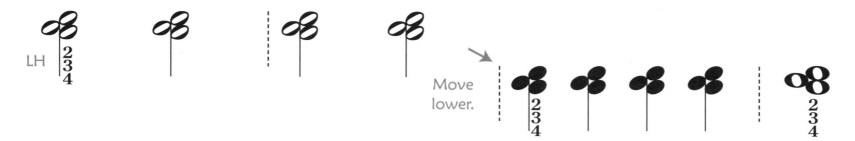

Pumping Iron (LH)

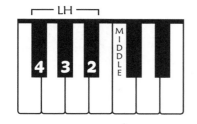

Play moderately loud.

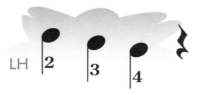

Move lower.

* Students should not hold down fingers that are not actively tapping. Holding down fingers may produce unnecessary tension in the arm.

6

Strong Fingertips (RH)

- Place the RH in a rounded hand position on the closed keyboard cover.

- Keeping each joint firm, imagine that your fingertips are very strong as you tap RH fingers 2, 3 and 4 on each fingertip pad.

- Start with finger 2 and tap each finger 4 times.*

Repeat 3 times each day.

Pumping Iron (RH)

Technique Tip: In "Pumping Iron (RH)," use *strong* RH *fingertips.* Use *arm weight* and *move freely* on the second line.

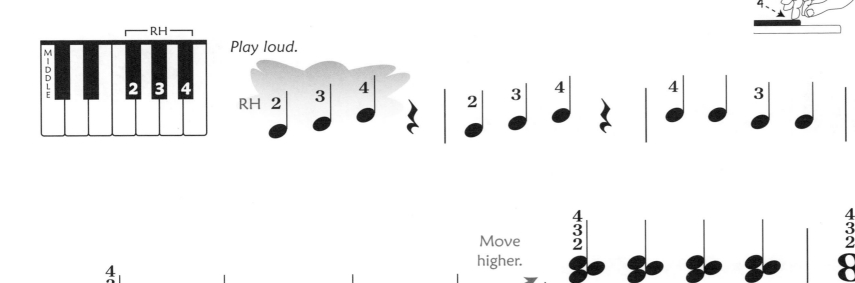

Play loud.

Move higher.

* Students should not hold down fingers that are not actively tapping. Holding down fingers may produce unnecessary tension in the arm.

Technique Tool 5

Finger Weights

- Place your LH in a rounded hand position on the closed keyboard cover.
- Imagine that each finger has a weight on its fingertip. Using fingers 2, 3 and 4, tap each LH finger *firmly* (𝒇) four times. Start with finger 2.
- Now imagine that the weight is no longer on each fingertip. Using fingers 2, 3 and 4, tap each LH finger *lightly* (𝒑) four times. Start with finger 2.
- Repeat with RH fingers 2, 3 and 4.

Repeat 3 times each day with LH, then RH.

Technique Tip: In "Balancing Weights," use *finger weights* and *arm weight* to create dynamics and a good tone at the piano.

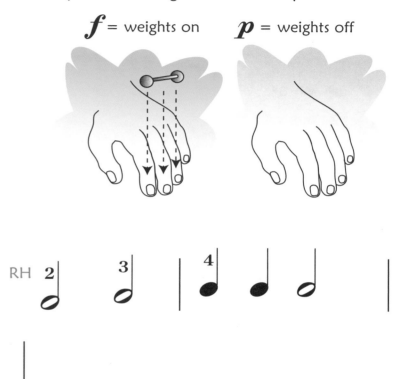

𝒇 = weights on   𝒑 = weights off

Balancing Weights

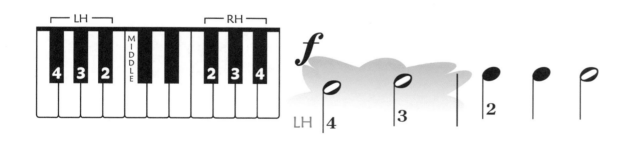

Artistic Etude 1

An etude is a study piece that helps improve technical and artistic skills. Discuss with your teacher where you will use *finger weights* and *arm weight* in this etude.

Bamboo Forest

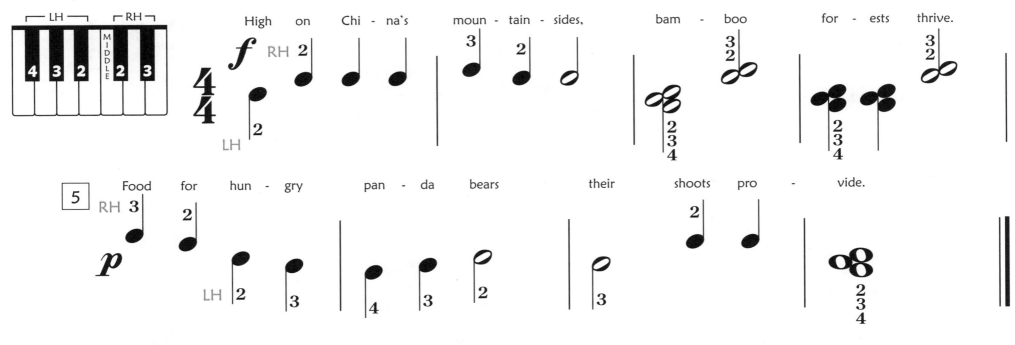

Duet: Student plays one octave higher.

Technique Tool 6

Repeated Notes

- On the closed keyboard cover, play "Close Call (LH)."
- When playing repeated notes, slightly lift the hand but keep the finger close to the key surface.
- Play "Close Call (RH)" on the closed keyboard cover. Stay close to the surface.

Repeat 3 times each day with LH, then RH.

Technique Tip: In "Close Call," stay close to the keys when playing *repeated notes*, and *move freely* up and down the keyboard. All repeated notes must be heard clearly.

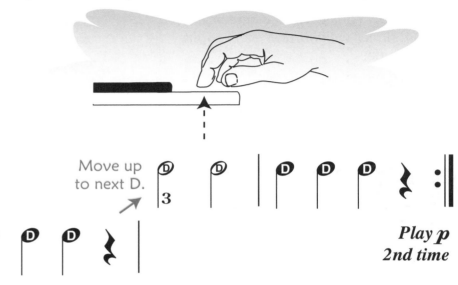

Close Call (LH)

Start low on the keyboard.

Play p 2nd time

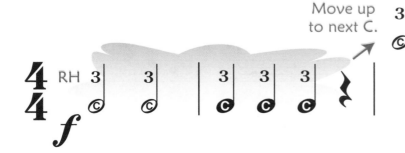

Close Call (RH)

Start in the middle of the the keyboard.

Play p 2nd time

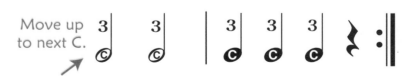

Technique Tool 7

Thumb Position

- Place the RH in a rounded hand position on the closed keyboard cover.
- Tap ♩ ♩ ♩ 𝄽 with energy using only finger 1 (thumb). Keep the thumb relaxed and the wrist loose as you tap on the *side tip.*

Repeat 3 times each day with RH, then LH.

✔ **Technique Tip:** In "On the Side," play on the *side tip* of the thumb. *Small finger weights* should be **on** when playing *mezzo forte* (***mf***) and **off** when playing *piano* (***p***).

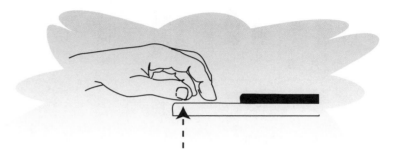

On the Side (RH)

Start on the highest E on the keyboard.

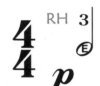

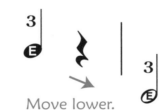
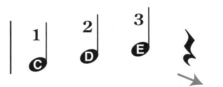

Move lower.

Play two more times.
Move lower each time.

On the Side (LH)

Start on the lowest E on the keyboard.

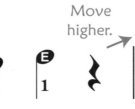

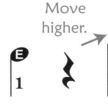

Move higher.

Move higher.

Play two more times.
Move higher each time.

Work It Out (LH)

✔ **Technique Tip:** Use **more** *arm weight* and *finger weight* as the music gets **louder.**

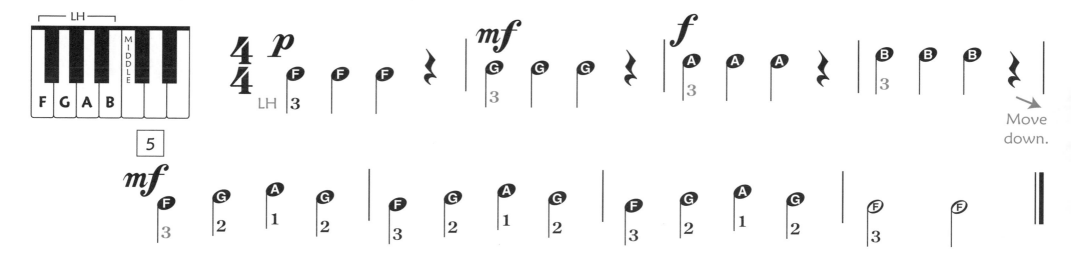

Move down.

Work It Out (RH)

✔ **Technique Tip:** Use **less** *arm weight* and *finger weight* as the music gets **softer.**

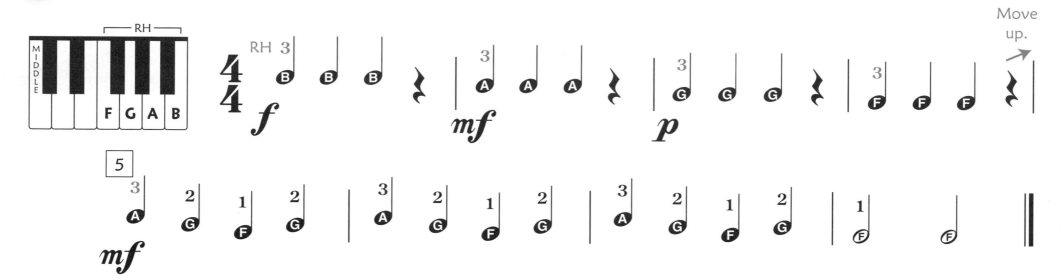

Move up.

Technique Tool 8

Finger Independence

- Play "Rise and Shine" on the closed keyboard cover, moving *precisely* from one finger to the next.

- Each finger should move *with energy*, keeping the joint closest to the nail firm.*

- Then play on the keyboard. Each note should sound clear.

Repeat 3 times each day.

Technique Tip: In "Rise and Shine," play each key with *finger independence*—precisely and with energy.

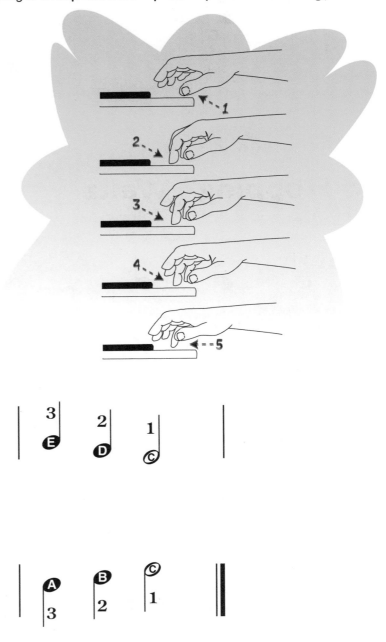

Rise and Shine

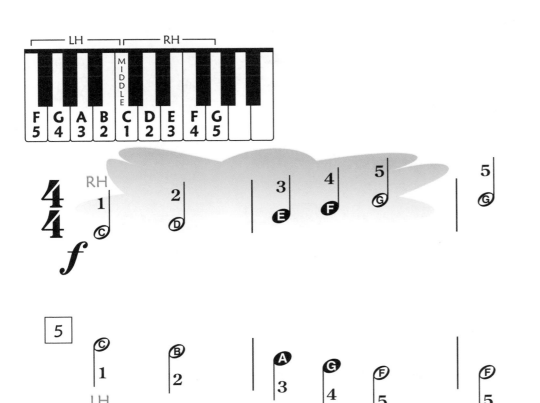

* Finger 5 is often the weakest finger. Students should keep this finger curved, the nail joint strong, and avoid playing on its side.

Lesson Book: page 28

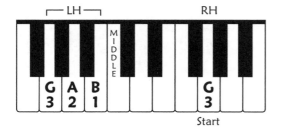

DANCE MARATHON

Playing Across the Bar Line

- On your lap, tap the rhythm of *"No Stopping" Waltz* with the correct hand as you count aloud.

- Keep a steady pulse throughout! Don't stop at bar lines.

- Beat 3 of each measure of *"No Stopping" Waltz* should go to beat 1 of the next measure without stopping.

Artistic Etude 2
"No Stopping" Waltz

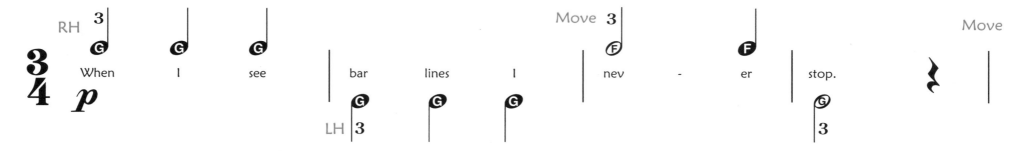

Duet: Student plays one octave higher.

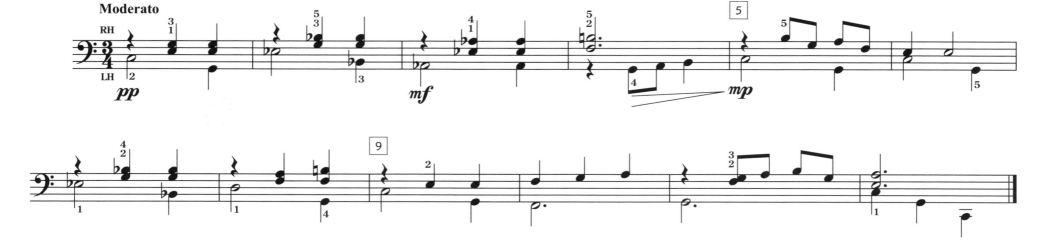

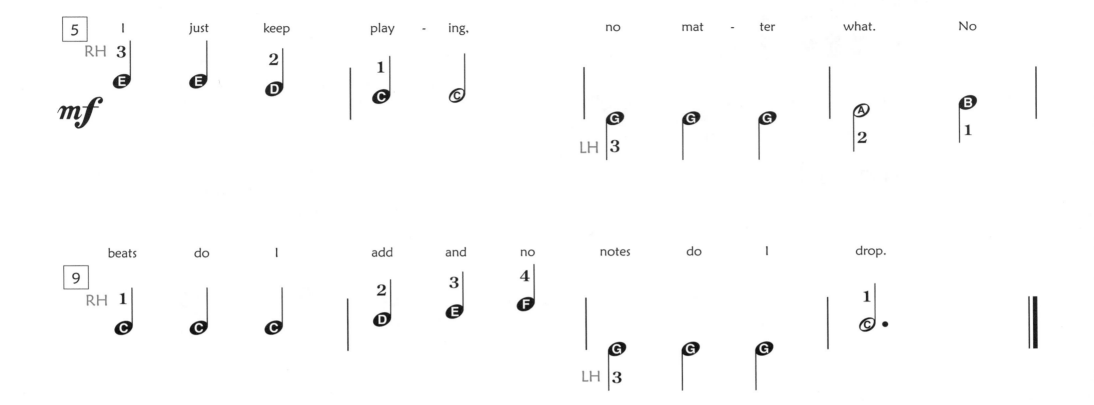

5 | I   just   keep   play - ing,   no   mat - ter   what.   No

9 | beats   do   I   add   and   no   notes   do   I   drop.

? Technique Quiz:

1. When playing the repeated notes in measures 1–3, keep the fingers close to *or* high above the keys.
circle one

2. When moving from one key to another, the fingers should play with energy. *or* with little energy.
circle one

16

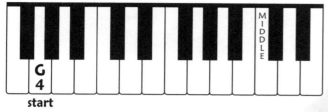

Patterns in Music

Often several notes or a rhythm in music will reappear later in the piece but begin on a different key. These notes form a *pattern*.

Up and Around

✔ **Technique Tip:** Memorize the pattern in measures 1 and 2, then play "Up and Around" from memory until the pattern changes in measure 15. Use *strong fingertips* and *finger independence*.

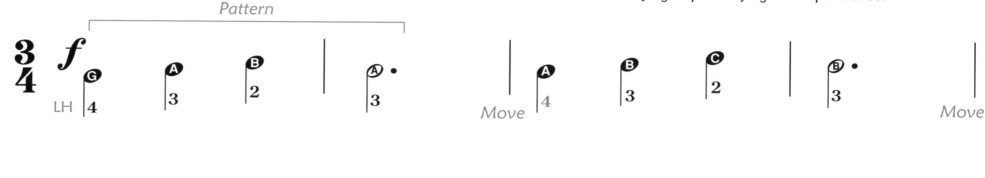

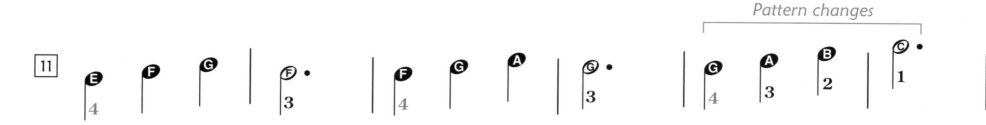

? **Technique Quiz:** How many times does the pattern shown in measures 1–2 appear in "Up and Around?" _____

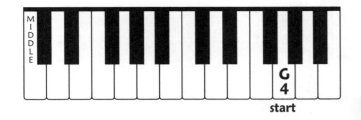

Down and Around

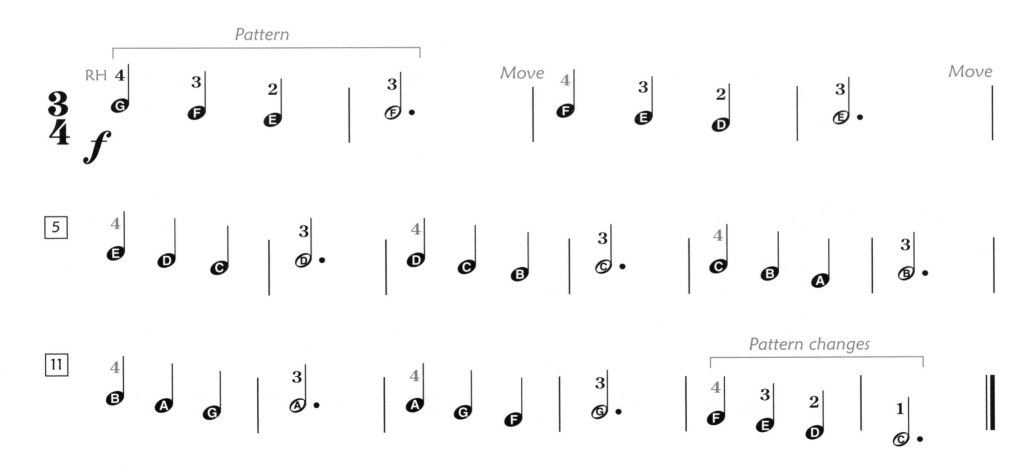

? **Technique Quiz:** How many times does the pattern shown in measures 1–2 appear in "Down and Around?" _____

Lesson Book: page 39

 Technique Tip: A round hand position will help build a strong bridge between fingers 1 and 5. In "Building Bridges," play on the *side tip* of the thumb and keep finger 5 curved. Use *arm weight* to create a full sound.

Building Bridges (LH)

Moderately

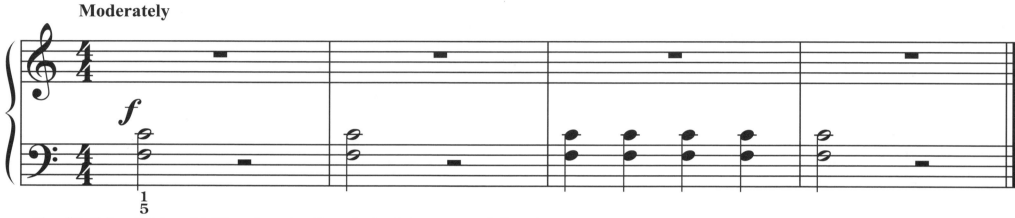

• Play "Building Bridges (LH)" again using **C** as the bottom note and **G** as the top note.

Building Bridges (RH)

Moderately

• Play "Building Bridges (RH)" again using **G** as the bottom note and **D** as the top note.

Lesson Book: page 39

 Technique Tip: In "Pumping Ivories," use *strong fingertips.*
Play on the *side tip* of the thumb and keep finger 5 curved.

Pumping Ivories* (LH)

Moderate waltz tempo

● Play "Pumping Ivories (LH)" on white keys moving **down** the keyboard (B, A, G) until you reach the next C with finger 5.

Pumping Ivories (RH)

Moderate waltz tempo

● Play "Pumping Ivories (RH)" on white keys moving **up** the keyboard (D, E, F) until you reach the next C with finger 5.

* Some pianos have white keys made of ivory and not plastic.

Lesson Book: page 41

Artistic Etude 3

Back and Forth

Playing Evenly from Hand to Hand

● Play "Back and Forth" on the closed keyboard cover concentrating on playing all notes in each hand with equal weight.

● Use *strong fingertips* as you play "Back and Forth" on the keyboard. When hands change, listen carefully to the first note played by each hand. These notes should not sound louder than the notes surrounding them.

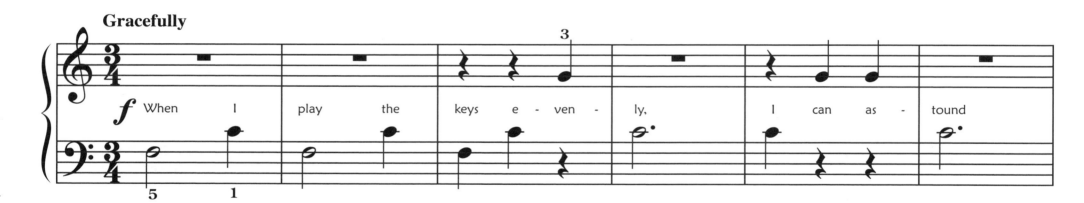

Gracefully

f When I play the keys e - ven - ly, I can as - tound

Duet: Student plays one octave higher.

Gracefully

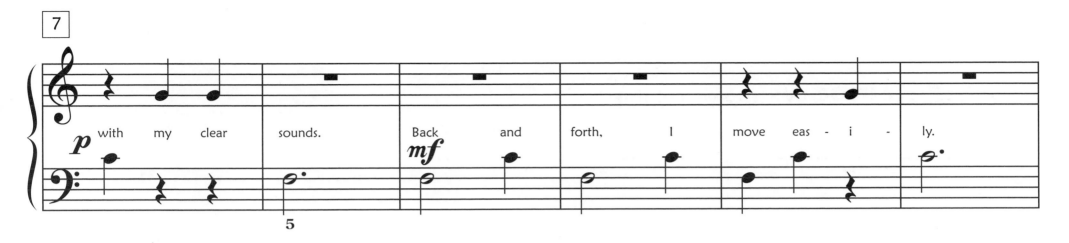

7

p with my clear sounds. Back and forth, I move eas - i - ly.

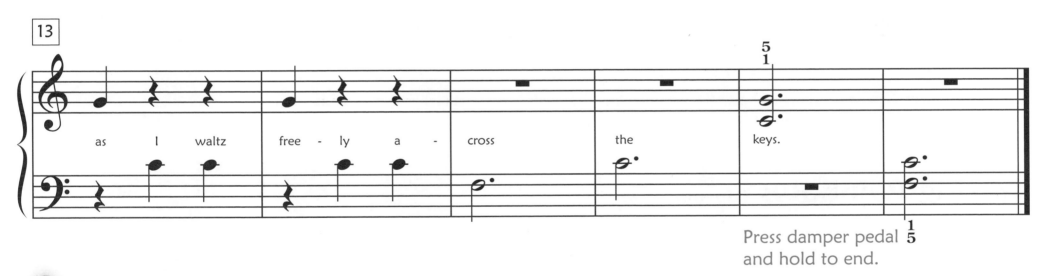

13

as I waltz free - ly a - cross the keys.

Press damper pedal $\frac{1}{5}$
and hold to end.

(?) Technique Quiz:

1. Arm weight is used in measures 17–18. The arms should feel

> light.
> *or*
> heavy.
> *circle one*

2. To keep a steady tempo,

> move without stopping
> *or*
> stop
> *circle one*

between beat 3 and beat 1 of each measure.

Technique Tip: In "Tracing Rainbows," stay close to the keys for the *repeated notes*. Move *freely* up and down the keyboard with curves like the arch of a rainbow.

Tracing Rainbows (Down and Up)

Gently

• Using RH finger 3, play "Tracing Rainbows (Down and Up)" beginning an octave higher than written.

Tracing Rainbows (Up and Down)

With confidence

• Using RH finger 3, play "Tracing Rainbows (Up and Down)" beginning an octave higher than written.

Lesson Book: page 45

 Technique Tip: Use *strong fingertips* and *finger independence* as you play "Falling Patterns" and "Rising Patterns."

Falling Patterns

Steadily, with energy

● Using the RH, play "Falling Patterns" an octave higher than written. Begin with finger 4.

Rising Patterns

Steadily, with energy

● Using the RH, play "Rising Patterns" an octave higher than written. Begin with finger 2.

Lesson Book: page 47

 Technique Tip: Use *finger independence* as you play each key precisely and with energy.

Keeping Fit (LH)

Moderately

Play "Keeping Fit (LH)" in the following ways:

- Begin on A and play only white keys.
- Begin on D and play only white keys.

5-Finger Fitness (LH)

Moderately

Play "5-Finger Fitness (LH)" in the following ways:

- Begin on D and play only white keys.
- Begin on G and play only white keys.

Lesson Book: page 51

 Technique Tip: *Finger weights* should be **on** when playing *forte* (f) and **off** when playing *piano* (p).

Keeping Fit (RH)

Moderately

Play "Keeping Fit (RH)" in the following ways:
- Begin on A and play only white keys.
- Begin on D and play only white keys.

 Technique Challenge: Play "Keeping Fit" hands together with the LH an octave lower beginning on finger 1.

5-Finger Fitness (RH)

Moderately

Play "5-Fitness (RH)" in the following ways:
- Begin on D and play only white keys.
- Begin on G and play only white keys.

 Technique Challenge: Play "5-Finger Fitness" hands together with the LH an octave lower beginning on finger 5.

Lesson Book: page 53

Playing with Dynamics

- As you play "Shades of Blue," imagine that each dynamic change is a different shade of the same color.

- For example, *forte* (***f***) notes are *navy blue*; *mezzo forte* (***mf***) notes are *medium blue*; *piano* (***p***) notes are *light blue*.

- Listen for different shades of blue as you play.

Artistic Etude 4

Shades of Blue

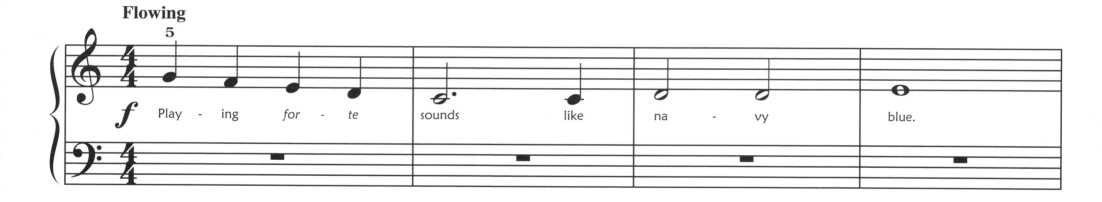

Duet: Student plays one octave higher.

5

mf Mez - zo for - te sounds like me - dium blue.

1

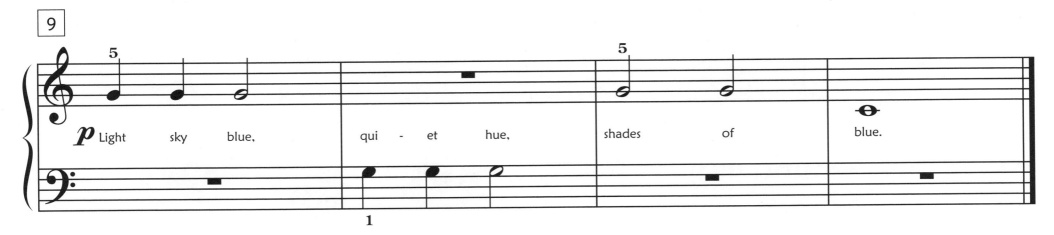

9

5   5

p Light sky blue, qui - et hue, shades of blue.

1

? Technique Quiz:

1. When playing *forte* (*f*) in measures 1–4, finger weights are   off.
   or
   on.
   circle one

2. When playing *piano* (*p*) in measures 9–12, finger weights are   off.
   or
   on.
   circle one

Technique Tip: *Small finger weights* should be **on** when playing *mezzo forte* (***mf***) and **off** when playing *piano* (***p***).

Weighting Around (LH)

Thoughtfully

• Continue moving down on white keys using this pattern, ending on C an octave lower than where you began.

Weighting Around (RH)

Patiently

• Start this pattern on the C above Middle C. Continue moving down on white keys using this pattern, ending on Middle C.

Technique Tool 9

Gentle Hand Rock

- Place the LH in a rounded hand position on the closed keyboard cover.
- Check to make sure that the wrist is level with the hand and arm, not dipping lower or rising higher.
- *Gently rock* the hand back and forth from finger 1 to finger 3.
- Feel how the weight shifts *slightly* from one finger to the other.
- Repeat with fingers 2 and 4.

Repeat 3 times each day, with LH, then with RH.

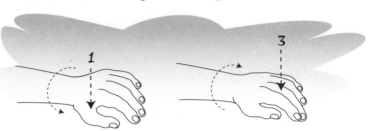

Technique Tip: In "Steady Rock," *gently rock* the hand from finger 1 to finger 3.

Steady Rock (LH)

Steady and gentle

• Repeat, using fingers 2 and 4.

Steady Rock (RH)

Steady and gentle

• Repeat, using fingers 2 and 4.

Lesson Book: page 60

Artistic Etude 5

Good Mood

Moods in Music

- Music can express many moods such as sad, happy, thoughtful or excited.
- Paint a sound picture of the mood as you play "Good Mood" by changing dynamics as indicated in the music.

Flowing

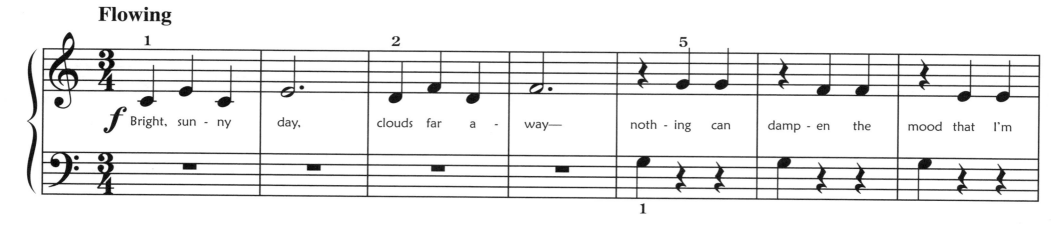

Bright, sun - ny day, clouds far a - way— noth - ing can damp - en the mood that I'm

Duet: Student plays one octave higher.

Flowing

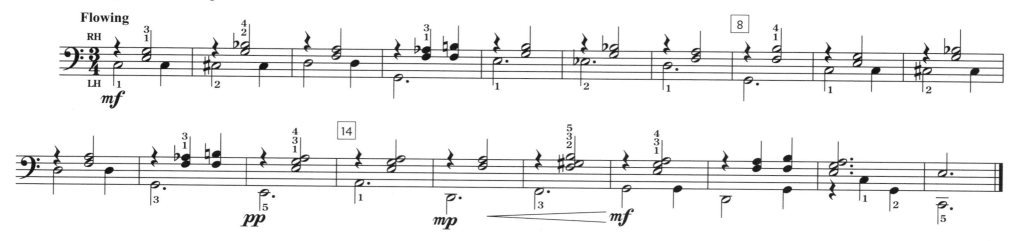

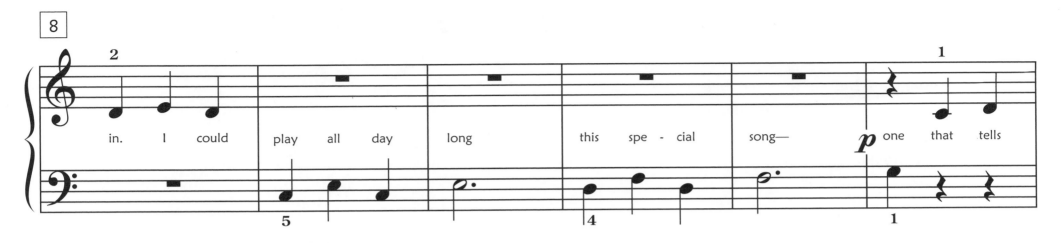

(?) **Technique Quiz:**

1. When playing measures 1–4, gently rock *or* steadily twist the hand as you move between the fingers.

   circle one

2. When moving from hand to hand, the first note of each hand should *or* should not sound louder than the notes surrounding it.

   circle one

Lesson Book: pages 62–63

Technique Tool Review

● Draw a line from the *Technique Tool* to its *matching description.*

Technique Tool	Description
Relaxed Shoulders	Arms feel relaxed and heavy as they drop.
Arm Weight	Move precisely from one finger to the next with energy.
Moving Freely	Play on the side tip.
Strong Fingertips	Finger joints are firm.
Finger Weights	Shoulders are in a natural position while playing.
Repeated Notes	Weights are on or off fingertips for playing f, mf or p.
Thumb Position	Fingers are close to the key surface.
Finger Independence	Hand moves back and forth to slightly shift weight from one finger to another.
Gentle Hand Rock	Hand and arm trace a gentle curved arch.